JOJO TALKS ABOUT
THE THREE BELL JARS

Mary Orelaru-Oyalowo

Halo
PUBLISHING
INTERNATIONAL

To Manny
From Grandpa &
Grandma

ISBN: 978-1-63765-168-1

Halo Publishing International, LLC
www.halopublishing.com

Printed and bound in the United States of America

Simplifying money management lessons for kids is a surreal and rewarding process. None of these would have been possible without some amazing people in my life.

I must thank God. Without Him, I wouldn't have been able to write this book.

I am grateful to my dear husband, Samuel. From being my sounding board to reading early drafts and giving me invaluable advice on the book. He played an important role in getting this book done. A special thank you to my children, Joanna and Eunice, for inspiring me to write this book. Many thanks to my parents and siblings for believing in me and supporting me. My beloved mother, Abioye, laid the foundation of the money management lessons I built on. My stepfather, Emmanuel, is one of my biggest cheerleaders. He is always there to cheer me on unconditionally. My siblings Tope, Segun, Dare, Adegboyega, and Abiola, read early drafts and supported me in bringing this book to life. It is because of my family's efforts and encouragements that I have a blueprint to pass on to children around the globe.

Thanks to everyone on my publishing team who helped me. Special thanks to Tosin Bashir, Ugochi Nmanze, Okeade Arts, and the Halo publishing team for their keen insights, editorial help, and support.

Contents

Meet Jojo

Hi! I'm Jojo, and I'm 4 years old.

I love my friends, and I love to talk about money and the best ways to use it!

My Dad and Mum say that we need money to buy things, like toys, food, and clothes.

Some people have a lot of money while some do not.

People with more money can buy more things, while those with less money cannot buy a lot of things.

Dad and Mum want me to know all about money and how to use it.

So, they are teaching me how to be a better money manager.

Want to know how?

I'll tell you how!

8

First, they gave me three bell jars for my birthday.

A green bell jar, a blue bell jar, and a yellow bell jar. Can you guess what the bell jars are for?

I will give you a hint: the value of money!

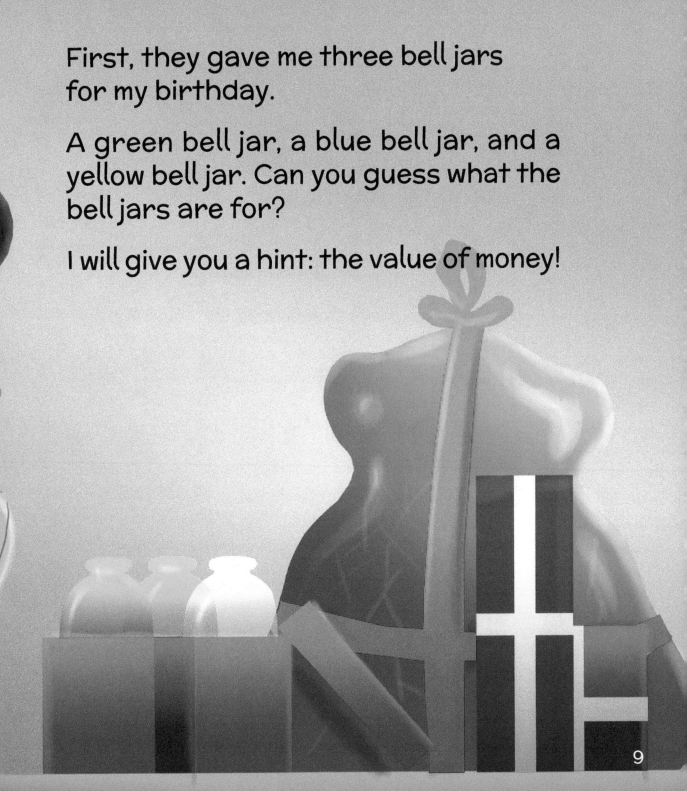

Dad and Mum got me the bell jars to teach me about money and how to manage it.

It was fun learning about money with my bell jars and I'm going to tell you all about it.

The green jar is for savings.
The blue jar is for spending.
The yellow jar is for sharing.

To use the jars, you'll split your money into three parts. Each jar gets one part.

12

First, I'll tell you all about the green jar.

The Green Bell Jar

The green bell jar is for saving.

You should put at least two dimes out of every dollar you receive, into the green bell jar.

It is smart to save part of your money in the green bell jar.

FUN FACT!

Green is the color of money and growth!

Dad and Mum say, "The more money that you save, the more your money grows bigger and bigger!"

What can we save money for?

We can save money for toys, chocolate, and books. People also save for school, vacations, houses, cars, and emergencies.

Mum says, "Having savings goals helps you know what you need and gets you closer to having them".

FUN ACTIVITY!

Write down the things that you want to *save* for.

TABLE TO LIST ITEMS

Are you still up for some more money-learning fun?!

Then let's go!

The Blue Bell Jar

Can you guess what the blue bell jar is for?

I will give you a hint: It makes you feel good!

The blue bell jar is for spending!

You should put at least seven dimes out of every dollar you receive into the blue bell jar.

The money in the blue bell jar is for buying the things you need, such as food, water, and clothes.

Dad also says that you can use the money in the blue bell jar to buy things you like, such as toys and chocolates.

Mmmm...yummy, I love chocolates.

24

Spending money on the things you need and like will make you feel happy!

Remember, when there is no money left in the blue bell jar, you have no more money to spend on things you need and like.

FUN FACT!

Blue is a color of responsibility.

Spending your money wisely means that you are responsible!

 Good money managers will only spend the money in their blue bell jar!

Do you think you could be a good money manager? Circle the emoji that represents your answer

Yes

No

FUN ACTIVITY!

Write down three things that you need and three things that you *want*.

TABLE TO LIST ITEMS

Now let's learn about the yellow bell jar.

Can you guess what it is for?

I'll give you a hint: It gives people hope!

The Yellow Bell Jar

The yellow bell jar is for sharing.

You should put a dime out of every dollar you receive, in the yellow bell jar.

Mum says, "Giving your money to charity or using it to buy things for those in need, is sharing".

Sharing what you have with others willingly is good.

FUN FACT!

Yellow is a color of hope and joy.

 By sharing your money with others, you give them hope and joy.

Dad says to remember to only share what is yours.

The money in the yellow bell jar is yours for sharing, and you can give some of it to the needy.

Sometimes, you might not feel like giving out something because you still need it.

Mum says that it is okay to feel this way, but if you can, share your money because it is kind to give.

Giving is paying forward every kindness that you have received!

I feel happy when I share by giving to the needy. Tell me how sharing makes you *feel*.

Write down the names of two people or charities that you would like to share your money with.

Now you know all about my three bell jars.

Sharing the money lessons I learnt from my Dad and Mum is fun and informative.

You can begin your money journey
today by getting three bell jars too!

Glossary

Charities [cheh-ruh-tees]: organizations that help and raise money for people in need.

Goals [gowlz]: Something you want and will work hard to achieve.

Growth [growth]: When something or someone gets bigger.

Hint [hint]: A clue to an answer or advice.

Informative [uhn-for-muh-tuhv]: Learning something important or useful.

Manager [ma-nuh-jr]: Someone who is put in charge, to take care of something or a place.

Receive [ruh-seev]: To be given something.

Responsibility [ruh-spaan-suh-bi-luh-tee]: Doing the things you are supposed to do.

Split [split]: to divide something into two or more parts.

Value [va-lyoo]: Something that is important to you.

Wisely [waiz-lee]: thinking and behaving intelligently.

CPSIA information can be obtained
at www.ICGtesting.com
Printed in the USA
BVHW021226240122
627017BV00007B/147

9 781637 651681